FILLING the MANGER

A Christmas Tradition of Spreading Kindness

JENNIFER CATNEY

Filling the Manger
A Christmas Tradition of Spreading Kindness
Copyright © 2023 by Jennifer Catney

Published by Lucid Books in Houston, TX
www.LucidBooks.com

All rights reserved. No part of this publication may be reproduced, stored in a retrieval system, or transmitted in any form by any means, electronic, mechanical, photocopy, recording, or otherwise, without the prior permission of the publisher, except as provided for by USA copyright law.

ISBN: 978-1-63296-615-5 (hardback)
ISBN: 978-1-63296-614-8 (paperback)
eISBN: 978-1-63296-616-2

Special Sales: Most Lucid Books titles are available in special quantity discounts. Custom imprinting or excerpting can also be done to fit special needs. Contact Lucid Books at Info@LucidBooks.com

For my mother, Odette,
who taught us the tradition

Each Year Before Christmas

at the start of December,
My mother did something
I'll always remember.

She'd take down a box
from a shelf
where she'd hide it
And open the lid to show
what was inside it.

Then she'd reach in and
carefully place on our table,
A small wooden manger
like you'd find in a stable.

She'd say, "This empty manger
will help to remind us
That the greatest of gifts is

THE GIFT OF GOD'S KINDNESS"

FOR ON CHRISTMAS

God sent us a gift
from above

His own baby, Jesus,

TO TEACH US TO LOVE

Then next to the manger she'd
place a small jar,
Filled overflowing
with pieces of straw.

She'd say, "We'll use this straw
to help us prepare,
To welcome the baby
and show that we care.

And for each act of kindness
we do every day,
Add a straw to the manger
where Jesus will lay.

By Christmas
our kindness will build

A SOFT BED

A place where the baby
can lay his sweet head."

So while we bake cookies
and hang Christmas wreaths
And decorate trees to
place gifts underneath

And dream of the presents
that we will soon find,
Remember to take time
each day to

BE KIND

Share kindness at school,
in your home, at the store.

to your neighbor,
hold open the door.

Set the table for dinner,
Pick up socks off the rug.

LEND ⋄A⋄ HAND

to your brother,

Give your
sister a hug.

SPEND TIME

with a friend who feels sad or alone.

SAY "I LOVE YOU"

to family who calls on the phone.

INVITE SOMEONE TO PLAY

with you,
share your best toys.

Give your parents a rest and an hour with no noise.

VOLUNTEER

to make lunches,

Paint someone a card.

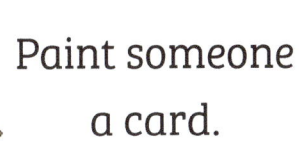

Help out a friend when their homework is hard.

TAKE CARE

of your pets, help clean up a spill.

Deliver A PRESENT

to someone who's ill.

Take the time to **JUST LISTEN** to someone's good news.

Say "God bless you," and "Thank you," and "I like your shoes."

There are so many
ways you can

BRIGHTEN EACH DAY

With the kind things
you do and the

KIND WORDS YOU SAY

Each night tell the story
of all you have done:

KIND ACTS
BIG AND SMALL

that you shared with someone.

Then for each
gift of kindness, for

FRIEND OR
FOR STRANGER

Take a straw from the jar
and place it in the manger.

With all of the kindness
and love that we bring,
We will build a soft bed

TO WELCOME THE KING!

By Christmas our manger will
be filled up with love
And ready for Jesus,
God's gift from above.

MAKE YOUR OWN MANGER

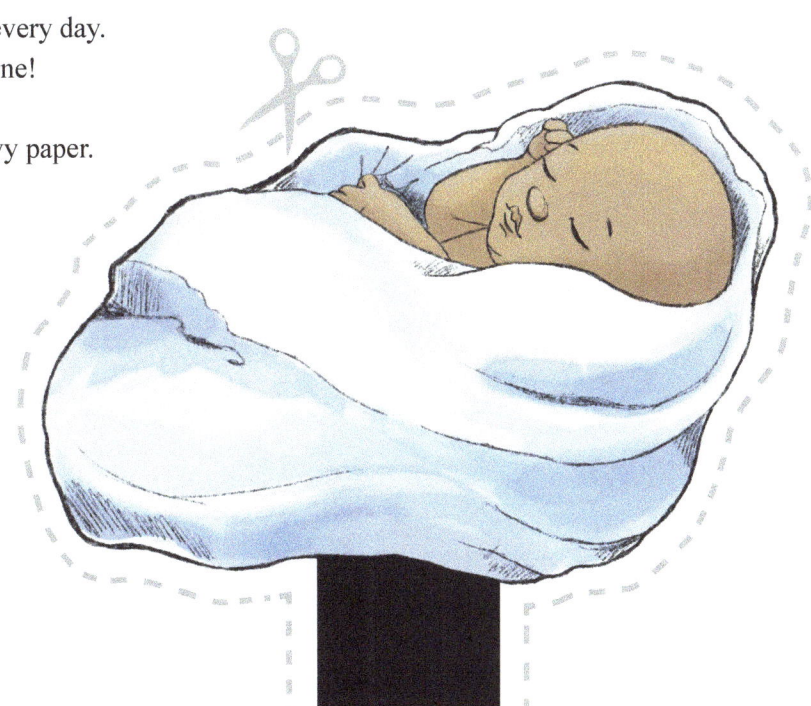

Fill your manger with daily acts of kindness.

You can use a brown paper lunch bag to make the manger. Cut off the top of the bag to make a manger about 3 inches high. Don't worry if you don't have real straw; there are lots of other things you can find around the house to use instead.

Some of the items we used include…
- curly ribbon
- yarn
- strips of yellow paper (slightly crumpled)
- shredded packing paper
- dry spaghetti noodles

Spread kindness by doing good deeds every day. Add a "straw" to the manger for each one!

Cut out the baby Jesus and glue to heavy paper. Add the baby to your manger on Christmas morning!

You can print more copies, including classroom sets, online at **www.fillingthemanger.com**

Be creative and share your manger and acts of kindness to inspire others! Help create a ripple effect of kindness that spreads throughout the world and lights the way for the coming of Christ.

Share your photos and stories with us on social media @fillingthemanger

ABOUT THE AUTHOR

Jennifer Catney is a storyteller, illustrator, and creator. She is passionate about spreading kindness and helping people recognize the power they have to make a positive difference in the world. Jennifer is a former elementary school teacher who now works as a geriatric Occupational Therapist. When she isn't creating, Jennifer loves to spend time kayaking, walking in nature, and making music with friends and family. Jennifer lives in Upstate New York with her family and their beloved cat, Auggie.

www.ingramcontent.com/pod-product-compliance
Lightning Source LLC
Chambersburg PA
CBHW060946100426
42813CB00016B/2875